Second Childhood

Books by Fanny Howe

POETRY

Eggs

Poem from a Single Pallet

Robeson Street

The Vineyard

Introduction to the World

The Quietist

The End

O'Clock

One Crossed Out

Selected Poems

Gone

Tis of Thee

On the Ground

The Lyrics

Come and See

Second Childhood

FICTION

Forty Whacks

First Marriage

Bronte Wilde

Holy Smoke

In the Middle of Nowhere

The Deep North

Famous Questions

Saving History

Nod

Indivisible

Economics

Radical Love: Five Novels

The Lives of a Spirit / Glasstown: Where Something Got Broken

What Did I Do Wrong?

ESSAYS

The Wedding Dress: Meditations on Word and Life

The Winter Sun: Notes on a Vocation

• *Second Childhood* •

Fanny Howe

• • •

GRAYWOLF PRESS

This publication is made possible, in part, by the voters of Minnesota
through a Minnesota State Arts Board Operating Support grant, thanks
to a legislative appropriation from the arts and cultural heritage fund,
and through grants from the National Endowment for the Arts and
the Wells Fargo Foundation Minnesota. Significant support has also
been provided by Target, the McKnight Foundation, Amazon.com,
and other generous contributions from foundations, corporations,
and individuals. To these organizations and individuals we offer our
heartfelt thanks.

Published by Graywolf Press
250 Third Avenue North, Suite 600
Minneapolis, Minnesota 55401

www.graywolfpress.org

Published in the United States of America

ISBN 978-1-55597-682-8

2 4 6 8 9 7 5 3 1
First Graywolf Printing, 2014

Library of Congress Control Number: 2013958013

Cover design: Kapo Ng

Cover art: Maceo Senna

Contents

Fear & hope are—Vision

WM BLAKE

Second Childhood

For the Book

Yellow goblins
and a god I can swallow.
Eyes in the evergreens
under ice.

Interior monologue
and some voice.

Weary fears, the
usual trials and

a place to surmise
blessedness.

The Garden

Black winter gardens
engraved at night
keep soft frost
on them to read the veins
of our inner illustrator's
hand internally light
with infant etching.
Children booked
on blizzard winds
and then the picture
is blown to yonder
and out of ink:
the black winter verses
are buds and sticks.

Parkside

Stone walls and chalk scratches
for different ages.

None of us could be sure now
how many we were or where.

There were hurtful pebbles,
cracked windows
and bikes. We cut the butter

and the day's bread evenly.
We were children and a metal bed.

　　　· • ·

Twelve loaves
and five thousand baskets.

Five baskets,
twelve pieces of dough.

Twelve times five and butter
for a multitude.

Bread made—that is—
with twelve thousand

inhalations of leaven.

My Stones

A pebbled island
is a kind of barge:
seaweed blackened
another glacial strand.

White quartz.

Some green mermaid's tears.

(A cask of bottles shattered.)

That home of mine
lost four inches
to erosion and great white sharks
but we kept floating.

I even found bedside stones
to play with in the night.

A colorful set to pretend
I could now see Ireland
from Boston.

Evening

Christmas is for children
on an English hill.
Simple, dismal,
and blissful,
a few little balls and crystal.
Dark by 4 p.m.
but you can ride your scooter
up the hill and down
in the arctic rain
each drop a dimple
on a—
and a silver handle
in a drain and a boy
can stand beside your hand
at the window
of a store full of cribs
and tinsel
before an icon

of the infant
with the news
rolled in his hand.

Xing

Odense is in Denmark and where are we now?
In a flying sleigh en route to Odessa.
The Black Sea is steaming below.

We sweep like snow-crystals every which way.
We who? My baby and me.
Off to the left, the sky is fleece.

In our warm sleigh and north of Norway,
away, away, what fun we are having!

More snow coming, more souls.
Baby lashes the dogs with a strand of her hair.
Her round face is circled with ermine.

Between Delays

You're like someone crossing a border daily
a person who is to itself unknown.

You're like a fragment that can't find what has lost it
or illuminate
what's going on or what it's seeing through.

Are we a child or a name?

John, John, John and John,
you're all so far from me.
Each like a walking stick inert
until picked up.

A person, the first I—
with few verbs left.

Vertical even when you laugh.

For Miles

Sunset in DC comes at 4:56.

This is nearly the same time as sunset in LA
when the El Royale sign lights up.

Sunset in Shannon comes several minutes earlier in
    the day.
Sunsets in Hong Kong and Havana are just about the
    same but far away.

Sunset in Chile and sunset in New Zealand
are only six minutes apart on different days.

The length of today in Boston is nine hours and
    fifty-one minutes.
The length of today in DC is ten hours and seven
    minutes.

I knew there was a difference between cities.
Don't worry. You didn't have to tell me about the
    bulge in the circumference.

If the light is shining in the House, Congress is still
     in session.
Of course the shape of earth is an oblate spheroid
wider in the middle by very few miles.

Even here on 21st Street, I can feel the sun moving
     in Vancouver.
There are twelve hours of light on one day in October.

I only needed to exist to know that the sun turns
     around the earth
and everything else at the center of the universe.

Loneliness

Loneliness is not an accident or a choice.
It's an uninvited and uncreated companion.
It slips in beside you when you are not aware that a
choice you are making will have consequences.
It does you no good even though it's like one of the
elements in the world that you cannot exist without.
It takes your hand and walks with you. It lies down
with you. It sits beside you. It's as dark as a shadow
but it has substance that is familiar.
It swims with you and swings around on stools.
It boards the ferry and leans on the motel desk.

Nothing great happens as a result of loneliness.
Your character flaws remain in place. You still stop in
with friends and have wonderful hours among them,
but you must run as soon as you hear it calling.
It does call. And you climb the stairs obediently,
pushing aside books and notes to let it know that you
have returned to it, all is well.
If you don't answer its call, you sense that it will sink
towards a deep gravity and adopt a limp.

From loneliness you learn very little. It pulls you
back, it pulls you down.

It's the manifestation of a vow never made but kept:
I will go home now and forever in solitude.

And after that loneliness will accompany you to
every airport, train station, bus depot, café, cinema,
and onto airplanes and into cars, strange rooms and
offices, classrooms and libraries, and it will hang near
your hand like a habit.
But it isn't a habit and no one can see it.

It's your obligation, and your companion warms itself
against you.
You are faithful to it because it was the only vow you
made finally, when it was unnecessary.

If you figured out why you chose it, years later, would
you ask it to go?
How would you replace it?

No, saying good-bye would be too embarrassing.
Why?
First you might cry.
Because shame and loneliness are almost one.
Shame at existing in the first place. Shame at being
visible, taking up space, breathing some of the sky,
sleeping in a whole bed, asking for a share.

Loneliness feels so much like shame, it always seems
to need a little more time on its own.

The Monk and Her Seaside Dreams

The monk is a single
and so am I
but which kind?

All of them
from young to wild
and the boyish one
(mine) cared for the weak
until there was no one
to care for him
besides an old woman
who lived as a she.

I became a penitent
sequentially:
first in sandals
then in boots
then with a hood
and bare feet.
Now night-bound, now nude, then old.

· • ·

Another brother and I took a train with a view of
    mountains
floating in water
out of Limerick Junction
to Heuston Station where Wittgenstein
tried to discover emotion.

He hit a horizon.

"Philosophy should only be written as poetry."

· • ·

In a Sabbath atmosphere you stand still and look
    backwards
for time has ceased its labors
and no cattle tremble.
You can contemplate the peripheries
and for a flash see the future as a field in a semi-circle.

Everything is even on the Sabbath. The died and the
    living.

Each person or place wants you as much as you want
    another.

                ·•·

Towards a just
and invisible image
behind each word
and its place in a sentence
we must have been sailing.

Scarcely defended, best
when lost from wanting perfect sense.
But still, recognizable.

Be like grass, the phantom told us:
lie flat, spring up.
Our veils were scrolls
you couldn't walk into
but only mark the folds.

                ·•·

I've lost my child at the bend where we parted.
We will never come back to that hour.

Let me write about the place again the path so sandy
and the table cloth blowing in a wind from
    Newfoundland.
It was here it began. She left her bouillabaisse
    untouched
and headed out on the train.
Sort of, soft, gold at sunset, turrets and sandals
were hard to identify so many copies.
Let me concentrate on ancestral faces
and I will recognize hers
before my powers fail and our DNA has been
    smeared
on cups and cigarettes, bottles and gloves, bowls
    and spoons
and replicated, sucked or kissed into the lips of
    strangers.

· • ·

I have to pass through the estuary
to investigate breakdown as a trail of nerve-endings
at the beginning of everything.

Scrapes like threads seeking holes.
It's a strange textile that serves as a road map.

This one did:
its blue led to the edge.

Where could a fabric begin and end except as a
    running woman
who sews and passes it along?
So I ran with it in my hands.

A kind of eucharist.
No break in its material from the first day on earth
to the Sabbath where all are equal
and the cows covered in sackcloth.

    · • ·

Where has my mind gone?

The bloody thieves
are very quick.

You may have noticed I'm naked
and sliced by glass.

Soon words will be disappeared
and then the Celtic church
and seven friends
I will not name.

One word that contains
so many:

dearth, end, earth, ear, dirt, hen, red, dish, it and
I must examine each part
then cut the ropes without a heart and set out.

　　　· • ·

The slide downhill on my back to a ledge
and the sea out there and a city
to the left of the mud.
The place they call an area
preparing for an earthquake. Under-shade and crowds
of hungry old people lining for bread.
One woman collapsed on her side
and another helped her up
and I was let into the bunker
by the best kind of communist.

There was orange vomit on a large cape over a large
    woman.

The hills! No bells.
I went down for what reason.
Not to enter a cell.

Luckily no one was white.
We discovered we were in a loft space from the
    olden days

that I indicated pleased me.
because I couldn't get my body out no matter what.

I paused long enough to encounter
a slender elder with the delicate posture of a
    Rastafarian.
The people were indifferent as they are to whites but
    polite.
The lean man showed me the door in colorful clothing.

But there was a huge blast from the building beside us
And we ran up rickety stairs to look at what
was now a structure speared with broken glass
    and stone.
A worker was already being transported on a stretcher.

We looked around at the mess then went inside
    to discuss
our love of failures, every one of us.

                · ● ·

I hauled so many children after me
with ropes and spears and nets
like sea-creatures that others would eat
without them I have no purpose.

As in the Gospel account, I believed in their belief.
But now there would be what? For he, the little one,
was kneeling and saying, You must run.

The lover I still loved stayed near the door
so I raced off, you stood, when the police came
seeking coherence in everything.

The total machine of retribution presses on.
Regardless of a prayer or what a person did.
This is incredible.
We're breaking up.

· • ·

A Trappist led me around as one of him
to a ship heading for the country where they edit the
    best films.
There was a city on deck: residential with pleasing
    evening trees
and then a downtown area until we couldn't tell
    the suns
from the portholes on board.

The ship would transport us to a staging dock in Iona.
I would lose my luggage from the twentieth century
(though its particles and buckles were forged in
    eternity)
and make my private vows to the creator
in every theater we entered.

                · • ·

Together we traveled in a boat as it filled with
    night-water
from the bottom up.

By night-water one means fear.
So the refilling is adding a sting to the salt.

Living naked
still leaves you covered

by a surface of wood, feathers, fur or skin.

Bare skin, blue skin: a muff of lambskin
over the ears where the thief can get in.

It's lucky the mind freezes before the heart.

· ● ·

Back there is the string of mountains your uncle
      painted
and you lost. Out there is the clotted cream
on a raspberry tart that he couldn't finish.

There is the goose and the blackbird, the brindled
      donkey

and the trap. They stand on the thin black thread of
   your lineage.
Your scissors are split, your fiddle is cracked, its
   strings are thin
and your mouth is dry, your clothes American.

No more rush of notes as if a window is open inside.

Only if you are insane or asleep
and the gods and animals
pound their way in
on a divine night wind.

Second Childhood

I have a fairy rosary called Silver who answers
questions when I dangle her in the sun at the window.
So I've asked her if I have a big ego and she swings
from side to side to say no.
We have other children for friends.
We don't understand why we are here in the world
with horrible grown-ups or what the lessons are that
we're supposed to learn.
It's not helpful for us to hear ourselves described in
religious, geriatric or psychological terms, because we
don't remember what they mean.
One cruel female said, "Don't laugh so much. You're
not a child."
My cheeks burned and my eyes grew hot.

I decided to stop becoming an adult. That day I chose to blur facts, fail at tests, and slouch under a hood. School was my first testing ground. I misunderstood lessons, assignments, meanings of poems and stories, and misinterpreted the gestures of characters in novels. I was awestruck by geology but mixed up the ages of rocks. I stared and giggled, and refused to take orders and was punished.

Throughout my life I have remained vague and have accepted the humiliation it brought, almost as if stupefaction were a gift. I willfully repeat my mistakes over and over and never learn from experience.

Every day has been a threat to this attitude so I avoid obligations.

For example, last night I dreamed I was on an airplane that was open to the sky and a storm was coming from a hive of stars, and I wanted to sit beside my daughter to watch the wind as we strapped ourselves tight to the invisible seats and stayed awake in the air.

If we had been grown-ups, we wouldn't have been able to see the stars or the storm. We would have perished.

So my commitment to childhood has once again been affirmed.

Read the signs, not the authorities.

You might think I am just old but I have finally decided to make the decision to never grow up, and remain under my hood.

We are like tiny egos inside a great mountain of air. Pressed upon by the weight of ether, we can barely breathe.

One ego is like a spider clutched to a web of its own making.

It turns to enamel and hardens on fulfillment.

Many egos fill up the whole body, every part to the tiniest hair.

Some egos are like fingernails that have been stifled by brittle paint.

All egos have something impersonal about them. They live deep inside like viruses and unlike gods who play in outer air.

But this ego covered my face with spider-dust as I lay in my bassinet.

Today I keep seeing gauze of a crystal kind, another kind of web of a type that doesn't harden but swings and shimmers.

It's the web-hood of a lost spirit.

At birth a baby failure is unconscious of the shadow
that covers her face: it's from the success leaning over
her crèche smudging out the color in her cheeks.
The failure is born to measure the shadow of
success. This is the failure's mission.
The secret hood around her face indicates her vocation.
The success arrives in triumph, and is instantly
obsolescent, while the failures keep trying, failing
and reproducing until another success is born. It
could be centuries from their lifetime.
It's NOT ironical but logical that the failure is the one
who recognizes success and identifies its potential in
her enemies.
She it is who keeps their egos alive with her tears.
She is their harshest critic, she who can separate the
fraud from the living, the cold from the lukewarm.
She is still a failure, a tiny ego who can't quite rise to
the occasion of being. She is driven by longing.
And she has crazy rules: "If your whole body can't
breathe the air, your prayers are incomplete. No nail
polish!"

I think the gods and goddesses were the last good grown-ups on earth. Once I saw them walking to a party along a beach and I could make out their shadows like a line of pines in an ocean breeze. They were laughing and calling to each other. Still they were always aware of their mortal children's prayers and answered them, sometimes in the form of mist, sometimes with needles of sunlight.

The gods existed outside the ego-world though they were certainly jealous and angry. Now some of them are pots and pans and wax and marbles, balls and kettles, rope and puddles. They emit a crackling sound when lightning hits the ground, and give people shingles. Other gods have chosen to break out to heaven where they blend into pastel and ride comets once a year. Sometimes it's hard to walk with so many gods bouncing around so I use a broom, rosary or cane to wave them away.

Progress

I have never arrived
into a new life yet.

Have you?

Do you find the squeak
of boots on snow

excruciating?

Have you heard people
say, It wasn't me,
when they accomplished
a great feat?

I have, often.
But rarely.

Possibility
is one of the elements.
It keeps things going.

The ferry
with its ratty engine
and exactitude at chugging

into blocks and chains.

Returning as ever
to mother's house
under a salty rain.

Slave up, slave down.

I want to leave this place
a postulant.
The gas stove is leaking
and the door of the refrigerator
stained with rust.
The mugs are ugly
and there are only two forks.
The walls are black
and soft, the bed a balloon
of night-clothing.
The stairwell sloped
to a dragger's pace.

There are big windows
with blind-slats dusty
and gray. Street life
goes all night and at dawn
freedmen shout and
laugh outside the kitchen.
Where does life begin?
In the lamb or in its threads?

If a man is numb
beat him.

If mute, shout
Say my name!

If he's still wearing
that coat, scream

Mercy, mercy!
and stroke it.

We drop the shadows where they are then
return to them
when the light has grown heavy.

You'll take your time lugging the weight into
        our room
or stand over there in the shade.

We've never been too sure that we exist as the
        earth does.
We're most at home in water
that soaks up the letters in our brains.

It could be we've been dry too long.

A spirit is a mess when excess spoils it.

I see them through the slats
and crack of the open window.
A cold rain. Leaves flipped
and palsied.

The river is brown near
the sand, loose banks and twigs
stick at the edge and a lilac's
silhouette of a dog.

How in the dark hole can I hide
if I can't get outside?

Then I won't remember
what I did to deserve it.

That arch and bridge
will form a shape of repentance.

If I'm hanging,
then judgment has been passed.

And I am hanging
upside-down
head swinging towards the moon.

Years of inversion.
A face in a mirror displaced
by its position outside silver.

And so?
Next will come muscle,
a little grief but no shoulder.

You're learning how to be a unit
with an infinite in its attic.

It's not difficult.
Light is the last message.

Then white streaks like oil paint
are the first to appear along the wet railing.

The ghost was soaked
and swelled into a human being
so close to resurrection
I could see the genius

of institutional religion.
Examine your conscience
until you are a postulant
who has only one sin to offer God.

Soon you'll wash that thing off
(scented by its parallel past) and pause.
What were your feet thinking in their hurry
to connect the parts?

Get the children to the other side!
What children? You were the one running.
There was never any other.

Now the sun is like a yolk that broke
into the corridor.
Sleepwalk through its gold
and you will see the original glitter
that lit our move to the lounge.

"I'm looking for a restaurant
with a baby spoon and knife."

"May I consult my psychic?"
A long shadow will mean your back's to the sun

and you can't empty the space you occupy anymore
expecting to see another opening.

The moods of strangers
determine your day.

Will the driver be kind?

Please God let him be.

This is poverty, not just
second childhood
in a divided city.

But my thanks to the soul-heat
of the one who works the register

and shakes the bag.

Infinite nesting pushes all matter
towards emptiness:
child-nodes,
tree-droppings
with a root element of null.
None is always included
in every cluster
of children.
Nothing in nothing
prepares us.

Yet a fresh light was shed
on immortality
for me climbing the stairs
firm foot first.

Everything was in the banister:
crows on branches, crickets,
architects, handsaws and democrats.
Red moon at 3 a.m.

Why Did I Dream

Why did I dream of Mohammed today?
Through the folding sheets he expressed his relief
that his words reached no modern critics.
He was, he said, only a poet.

I think I know what he meant
like the Uzbek scenes
that make up that whole trilogy by Ali Khamraev.
The robot that Nebuchadnezzar owned
was hard to pull apart or analyze without ruining
each click.
A series of scenes that could never take place
might drive people to theorize.

I tried the night after
but woke up struggling with machines
a helpless elder with fingers too weak to bend the bits
    around the neck.

Flame-Light

In Anatolia (where I've never been) the saffron hills
    seem to border
an ocean and the orange car lights mime the same
    in the sky.

A hospital and autopsy room and the body are being
    ripped apart without respect:

A heart slapped in a bucket: dirt in the trachea
    and lungs.
A hospital worker was better than a physician to
    the body.
Good with her hands in a bucket
like a worker at the till in a supermarket.

She said we have everything in reverse.

As an example a red corpuscle flew from the corpse
onto the collar of the detective
who could name the properties in a drop of blood
and this way prove there is no God.

The Cloisters

You stand with the rest of the children holding hands.

Your little aunt with a fox-skin on her shoulder is
    showing you
unicorns in a tapestry and the words:

"Please wash and love me."

Did she go to heaven when the membranes
of The Book were flipped

by the wind on the hospital roof?
She wanted to, and not.

Smoke from the vent gray sheets on which some days
    are written
flew apart in entropy's tendency towards a disorder
    seemingly insane.

Angelopoulos

Pulpy islands streak the fog and unify the effect
   of gray.
Even electric lights have contours of shade
because there's too much stuff from the recent past,
a gray glassiness behind every lens.
Silver is always weak.
Three church spires in one little city pebbles of rain.
Again, the electric lights: in a strand like citrine.
Globs of errors open for the two
gay guys railing markers over wet piers.
A sick flag buffers in air. Why is the boy dancing?
He's white and seems to want attention.
But it's the fatherless children the father follows.

Sometimes

Sometimes a twinkle
gets in my eyes.
It's like a rhinestone
on a prom dress.

It shoots light
so bright I can't blink
without tears.
If I pump my temples

with my fists
and close my eyes
it reddens in blood.
This is only one possibility

besides the metaphysical.
Sometimes it's
a prick of sweat
or a word or a prophet

sweating at a bus stop.
There are gangs
who would kill to know what to name
such a gem because there is none.

A Child in Old Age

Every room is still a mansion to you:
you who wants to live in an Irish hotel!

To sit in a lobby beside the fire with your feet
    in a chair.

To stare at the other children seeking asylum.

        · • ·

Your brain is a baby.
And all the ancients are in it still.

Your heart is a channel
and a crib for them.

They rarely come down

or out in the light
but steer you awkwardly with their cries.

Your brain is still becoming
an independent being

while your heart always needs air.

　　·•·

I had an infant who was an orphan who lived
　　between my ears.

Its sobs could only be heard
when it circled the pump.

How it hurt!

Another infant lived like an octopus fully exposed
with a skull like a bottle cap inside its thought.

It was the arms of my heart.

A heart is a mind that's only trying
to think without an unconscious.

The tentacle is a brain too.

And its adaptable jelly's
just as intelligent as human blood.

Sometimes you look into a baby's eyes.

"Bless her," you suggest to passersby
yourself being old and unnecessary.

But no one does.

Please, you beg. The tears of an infant can be bottled
      and hidden
for special occasions.

One drop on your tongue and you won't ask for more.
You've thought this somewhere before.

Born Below

Born below a second time.

The shade of the first cast across and down.

Never shakes it off.
Her mouth.

"Don't smile. It's ugly. You'll get lines."

The shade symbolizes an object in front of the sun:
a blotted person
and subversion.

Her hand over her eyes indicates she herself is
    blocking the light.

Never the best.

The best has good taste and self-preservation, pride
    in property.

What will we do with the others?

    · • ·

She grows very little without light but stays weak
(and hangs at the apartment window

lacking attention doesn't adapt).

She's a midget in a mighty nation.
An eclipse of the face.

What could be the value of being shaded
in broad daylight.
Of being aged in the night.
Of learning the secular rule of life.

The Coldest Mother

I can only follow one stone through
to its interior: and I do.
An amethyst from Achill.
The stone is transparent violet.
Firelight plays with its color the way eyes play with
    tears.
It's cold where east is north and the earth is flat
and a person grows old.
Equivalence—no matter at what distance.

The fluttering snow is at the mercy of
ever-increasing crescents crossing circles
measured by squares, dashes,
fish bladder, almond patterns, placenta.
The folks up higher know everything of illness.
I saw a child rolled in a cloak of snow
to kill his fever.

Irregular heart, aortic stenosis,
rheumatism, atrial fibrillation, vertigo, blood clots,
deafness, colitis and poor eyesight.

Scars on a wrist and internal stitches,
headaches, PTSD from winter accidents,
childbirth. Sorry, this is ordinary
stuff for a cold mother. At the end
she wants to live in comfort like a pearl in an oyster.
She can chill here in peace and suck on ice.

The sun is warm, the northern lights are curtains
blowing across the heavens to which I float.
Every faraway ice floe leads to fairies.
And every boat leads to material sciences.
I know about both of them
and I still believe they're too much alike.

White icebergs float or sink
under the wings of Aer Lingus.
Bling wobbles on a window:
it's the sun our beloved.
See the monk on the Skellig squeeze and rub
his frosty eyes
when he spots twelve swans

and a little girl
on a purple amethyst in the ocean foam.

· • ·

An early scene
innerly seen:
random sprays
of snow across Fresh Pond
(far below freezing
in Fahrenheit)
could be a white man's torso
who escaped a hospital
and shed his sheet and slid
happily face down on a mud-streaked mass
of ice. Could be cyclamen
with its leaves like violets
or refugee camps in Syria.

I must not lose heart.
It takes sixteen years for

a soul to cross the silvery ice
to the forbidden fields of grace
never knowing if it's fair
to choose self-starvation over health care.
I was such a cold mother a mineral was a flower.

Dear Hölderlin

(for Maureen Owen)

Years ago in a migration
we each carried our own
rug and pillow,
telescope and strings.

Our tent was portable and able
to be dismantled.
It could be rolled
and stuffed very fast.

Flowers and grass
still grew freely and sea-lilac
had already cracked
the tarmac. So there was sustenance.

At the estuary nearby
two continents had split apart
and a curlew
flew alone and crying.

Carefully a book
would be buried
with iodine and wine
and food that doesn't rot.

The cross is a good marker
for an avenue and white clover,
trampled where little
sweet pea is growing higher.

Down the hill comes a poet
with ginger hair, he puts
violets inside his hat,
herbs and water and says:

There was once music here,
a round table
and gang prayer,
and an exploding glacier.

Women kept each tent clean
until one cried,
I'm going to take care
of myself.

We heard her packing
the woods into her tote
like a nymph
managing a shipwreck.

After that, for us all
empathy was our only hope.

A Vision

Some old people want to leave this earth and
experience another.
They don't want to commit suicide. They want to
wander out of sight
without comrades or luggage.

Once I was given such an opportunity, and what did
I find?

Mist between mountains, the monotonous buzz of
farm machinery,
cornstalks brown and flowers then furrows
preparing to receive seeds for next year's harvest.

A castle, half-ruined by a recent earthquake still
highly functional.
Computers, copying machines and cars.
It was once a monastery and home for a family
continually at war.
Cypress trees and chestnut and walnut trees. A swing
hanging long from a high bough,

where paths circle down, impeding quick escapes by
armies or thieves.

I was assigned the monastic wing that later became
a granary.
Brick-red flagstones, small windows with hinged
casements
and twelve squares of glass inside worn frames.
From the moment I entered the long strange space,
I foresaw an otherworldly light taking shape.
Scorpions lived in the cracks.

I came without a plan, empty-handed except for my
notebooks from preceding days.
This lack was a deliberate choice: to see what would
be revealed to me by circumstances.

I took long walks that multiplied my body into
companionable parts.
Down dusty roads and alongside meadows,

and pausing to look at the mountains and clouds,
I talked to myself.

Mysticism "provides a path for those who ask the way
to get lost.
It teaches how not to return," wrote Michel de Certeau.

   · • ·

One day I had the sense that there were two boys
accompanying me everywhere I went.
I could not identify the boy on the left,
but the one on the right was overwhelmingly himself.
Someone I knew and loved.
The other one was very powerful in his personality,
an enigma and a delight.

His spirit seemed to spread into the roads and
weather.
Silver olive trees and prim vineyards.

Now a rain has whitened the morning sky but every
single leaf holds a little water and glitter.

· • ·

Mirror neurons experience the suffering that they see.
A forest thick with rust and gold that doesn't rust.

I saw a painting where the infant Jesus was lying on
his back
on the floor at the feet of Mary
and his halo was still attached to his head.
And another painting where there were about forty
baby cherubs
all wearing golden halos. Gold represents the sun as
the sun represents God.

Outside wild boars were still roaming the hills.
Maize, sunflowers, honey, thyme, beans, stones,
olives and tomatoes.
Rush hour in the two-lane highway.
Oak tree leaves curled into caramel balls.

A Franciscan monk sat on a floor reciting the rosary,
a concept borrowed from Islamic prayer beads
centuries before.

Figs, bread, pasta, wine and cheese.
These are not the subconscious, but necessities.
People want to be poets for reasons that have little to
do with language.
It is the life of the poet that they want, I think.
Even the glow of loneliness and humiliation.
To walk in the gutter with a bottle of wine.
Some people's lives are more poetic than a poem
and Francis is certainly one of these.

I know, because he walked beside me for that
short time
whether you believe it or not. He was thirteen.

That night I drank walnut liqueur, just a sip, it tasted
like Kahlua.
The inner wing of a bird is the color of a doe.

And the turned-over earth is the color of a nut, and
a bird,
but soon it will be watered for the green wheat of
spring.

Flying up the hill on the back of the motorbike in the
warm Roman air was like drinking from the fountain
of youth.

Umbrella trees along the Tiber.

I walked on the rooftops across Rome, including a
grassy one, and one where a palm grew out of a crack
in the rocks.

I was carrying an assortment of envelopes containing
paintings and notes for my Mass but they could not be
managed easily because their shapes were irregular.
Some had juttings, some were swollen, the color red
was prominent. They depicted divided cities, divided

into layers, not all in a line. A layer cake sagging under
the weight of accumulated dust, dirt and now grass.

Each layer had been purchased at the cost of decades,
even centuries of hand-hurting, back-breaking slave
labor. *Caveat emptor!*
Broken columns, mashed marble friezes and faces. The
triumph of greed
was written across my storyboard. The city was a
mighty and devouring creation,
a creature with a crusted skin.

Even in the city you look for a place that welcomes
you. You actually want to be found!
Being found is the polar opposite of making a vow.
You are a pot of gold and not the arc of the rainbow.
When you sit down on a stone, face up to the sun, you
can't help but think, *Mine, mine.*
And you don't have to promise anything to anyone
in time.

You may be called to a place of banality or genius,
but as long as it is your own happiness that responds
to it,
you are available to something inhuman.
Mozart sat at the piano for the better part of every day.

All over the world monks have lived in desert hovels
as scribes, prophets, mendicants.
They are the extreme realization of one aspect of
human personality
that tends towards lack of possession and solitude.

There was a hole in the roof of the Pantheon where
we were told
that the snow fell through onto the relics of Catherine
of Siena
the mystic and onto the porphyry.

A man in Rome told me that a monkey climbed down
a wall

holding an infant in his arms and in remembrance
there is a statue of the Madonna
on the very rooftop where he began his descent.

Alas

For you, what is happiness?

Black tiles and slant
of ribbed clouds.

A child's rainbow
with a house under it.

Clothes in the washer
clapping all night.

Acknowledgments

Thanks as ever to the editors of Graywolf Press and to the staff and atmosphere of the Vermont Studio Center and to the kind people of Civitella Ranieri. For help along the way, my thanks to Rae Armantrout, Christian Wiman, William Corbett, Carolyn Forché, Isaac Slater, Richard Kearney, Elizabeth Robinson, Linda Norton, Carmine Cerone, Xandra Bingley, Lynn Christoffers, and to the exemplary life of Joeritta de Almeida.

I would like to thank the editors of the following publications that published my poems and the poems of so many others:

American Poet, The Baffler, Consequence, The Economy, Epiphany, Fact-Simile, Fire (UK), *Golden Handcuffs, The Harvard Review, The Lamb* (Song Cave chapbook), *New Orleans Review, Pataphysics, Paul Revere, Plume, Poetry, The Straddler, Talisman, The Volta,* and *Water~Stone Review.*

Fanny Howe is the author of more than twenty books of poetry and prose, including most recently *Come and See, The Lyrics,* and *The Winter Sun: Notes on a Vocation.* She received the 2009 Ruth Lilly Poetry Prize from the Poetry Foundation for lifetime achievement, and she has won the Lenore Marshall Poetry Prize from the Academy of American Poets and the Gold Medal for Poetry from the Commonwealth Club of California. She lives in New England.

The text of *Second Childhood* is set in Minion Pro, an original typeface designed by Robert Slimbach in 1990. Book design by Ann Sudmeier. Composition by BookMobile Design & Digital Publisher Services, Minneapolis, Minnesota. Manufactured by Versa Press on acid-free, 30 percent postconsumer wastepaper.